Iowa

BY K. A. HALE

An Imprint of Abdo Publishing
abdobooks.com

abdobooks.com

Published by Abdo Publishing, a division of ABDO, PO Box 398166, Minneapolis, Minnesota 55439.

Printed in China.
052024
092024

Cover Photo: Grindstone Media Group/Shutterstock Images
Interior Photos: Aaron Yoder/iStockphoto, 4–5, 29 (bottom); Grant Wood/GraphicaArtis/Archive Photos/Getty Images, 6; Danita Delimont/Shutterstock Images, 8 (top left); Shutterstock Images, 8 (top right); Anzhela Shvab/Shutterstock Images, 8 (bottom left); iStockphoto, 8 (bottom right), 16; Nancy Bauer/Shutterstock Images, 10; Zack Frank/Shutterstock Images, 12–13; Madeleine Openshaw/Shutterstock Images, 15; Kevin E. Schmidt/Quad-City Times/Zuma Press, Inc./Alamy, 18; Jacob Boomsma/Shutterstock Images, 20–21, 26; Science History Images/Alamy, 23; Clint Farlinger/Alamy, 25, 28 (bottom); Joe Taylor Cinema/Shutterstock Images, 28 (top left); Red Line Editorial, 28 (top right), 29 (top)

Editor: Marley Richmond
Series Designer: Katharine Hale

Library of Congress Control Number: 2023949343

Publisher's Cataloging-in-Publication Data

Names: Hale, K. A., author.
Title: Iowa / by K. A. Hale
Description: Minneapolis, Minnesota: Abdo Publishing, 2025 | Series: Discovering the United States | Includes online resources and index.
Identifiers: ISBN 9781098293857 (lib. bdg.) | ISBN 9798384913122 (ebook)
Subjects: LCSH: U.S. states--Juvenile literature. | Iowa--History--Juvenile literature. | Midwest States—Juvenile literature. | Physical geography--United States--Juvenile literature.
Classification: DDC 973--dc23

All population data taken from:
"Estimates of Population by Sex, Race, and Hispanic Origin: April 1, 2020 to July 1, 2022." *US Census Bureau, Population Division*, June 2023, census.gov.

CONTENTS

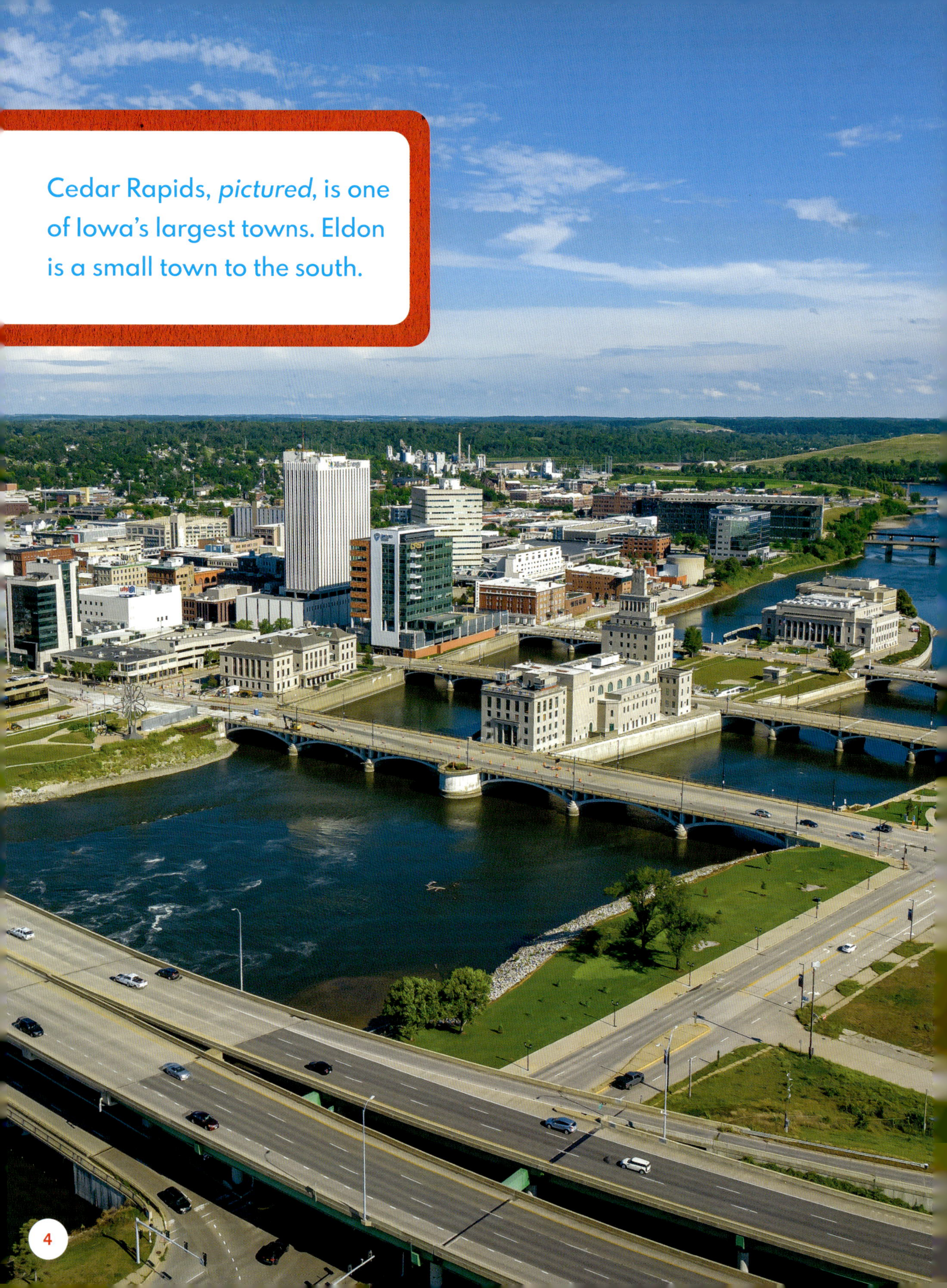

Cedar Rapids, *pictured*, is one of Iowa's largest towns. Eldon is a small town to the south.

CHAPTER 1

American Icon

In 1930, Grant Wood was visiting Eldon, Iowa. Wood's art skills were well-known in his hometown of Cedar Rapids, Iowa. The owner of a Cedar Rapids art gallery was hosting an art show in Eldon. He asked Wood to come for the show.

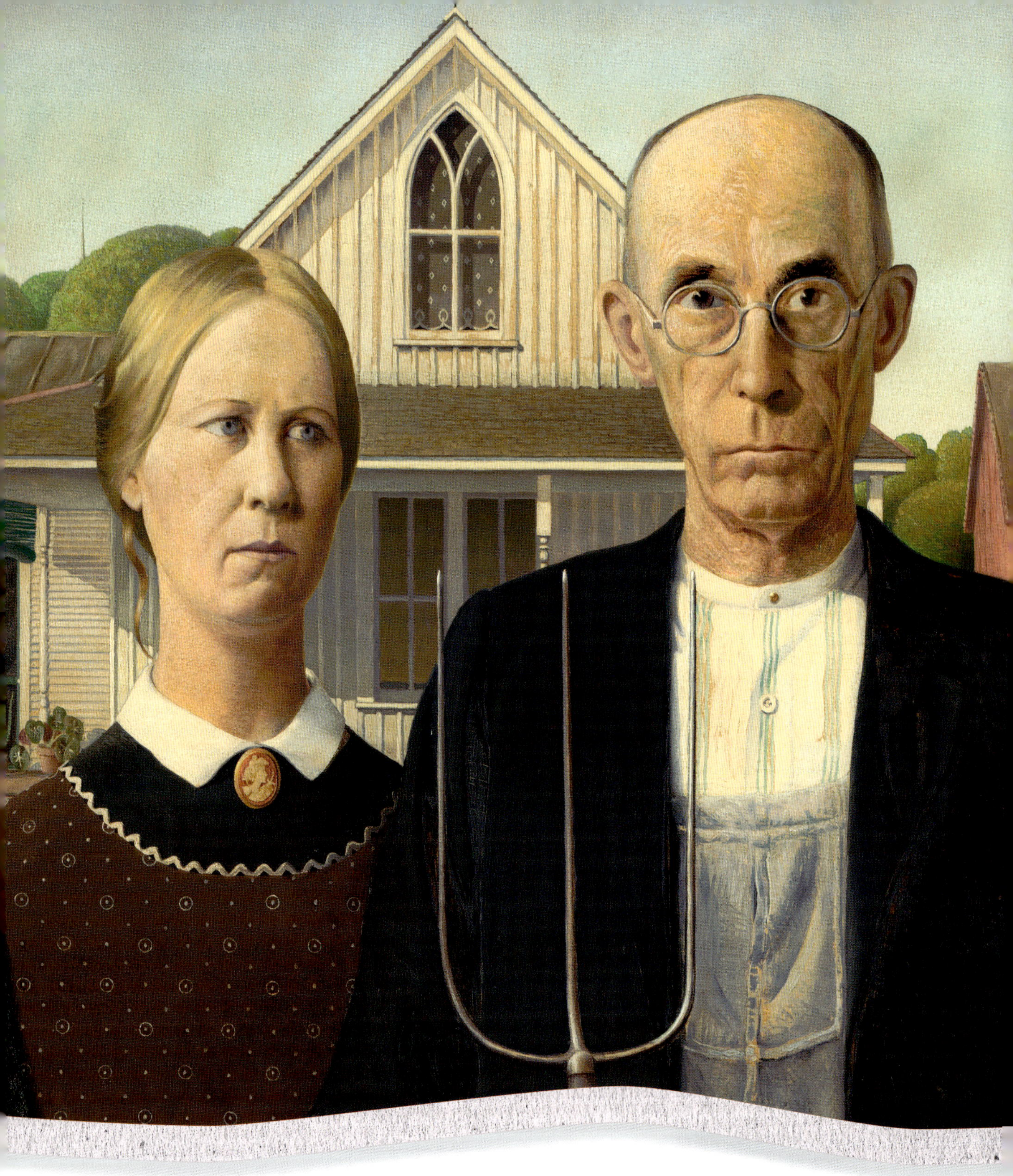

The Art Institute of Chicago bought *American Gothic*. The painting remains on display there.

While driving through town, a house caught Wood's eye. The house was small and plain. But the upstairs window stood out. It was grand. Wood was inspired. Later, he asked his sister to pose for a painting. He convinced his dentist to model too. Wood painted them standing in front of the house wearing old-fashioned clothes.

The house was built in the Carpenter Gothic architectural style. This style featured fancy details on plain houses. Wood called the painting *American Gothic*. Soon the painting became famous throughout the country. Wood painted many Iowa scenes throughout his career. But *American Gothic* was his most famous work. It is one of the most famous pieces of American art.

Iowa Facts

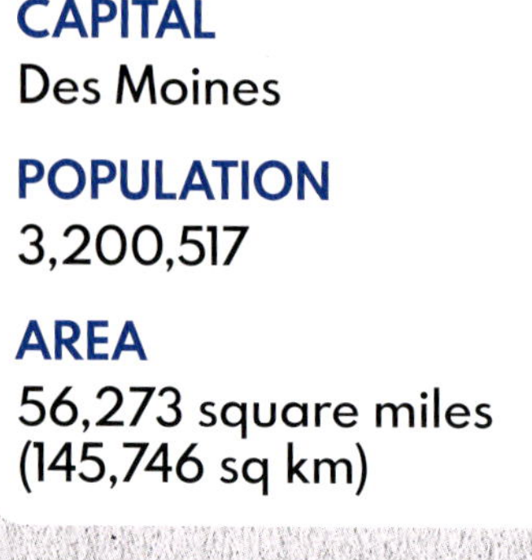

DATE OF STATEHOOD
December 28, 1846

CAPITAL
Des Moines

POPULATION
3,200,517

AREA
56,273 square miles (145,746 sq km)

STATE BIRD

Eastern goldfinch

STATE TREE

Oak

STATE FLOWER

Wild rose

STATE ROCK

Geode

Each US state has a different population, size, and capital city. States also have state symbols.

Wood's Homeland

Grant Wood found beauty in Iowa's landscapes.

Most of Iowa's land is used for farming.

Forests and rolling hills are found throughout the state. Iowa is also home to **bluffs** and prairies. Native prairie plants can survive Iowa's extreme weather. Iowa has hot, **humid** summers. The winters are cold and snowy.

Butterflies and other insects make their homes in prairies. So do many other animals. Deer and foxes run through Iowa's forests.

Prairie Restoration

Up to 80 percent of Iowa's land was once prairie. But prairies were destroyed to build cities and farms. Today, less than 0.1 percent of Iowa's prairie remains. The Prairie Resource Center provides seeds for native prairie plants. These seeds are planted on public lands. Other organizations help protect prairies in the state.

The Mississippi River flows along Iowa's eastern border. Wisconsin and Illinois are on the other side.

Bald eagles, ospreys, and eastern goldfinches fly through the skies. Iowa's lakes and rivers are home to fish, otters, turtles, and swans.

Iowa is in the Midwest. Minnesota borders Iowa to the north. Wisconsin and Illinois lie to the east. Missouri is Iowa's southern neighbor. South Dakota and Nebraska border Iowa to the west. The Missouri River creates Iowa's western border. The Mississippi River is the eastern border.

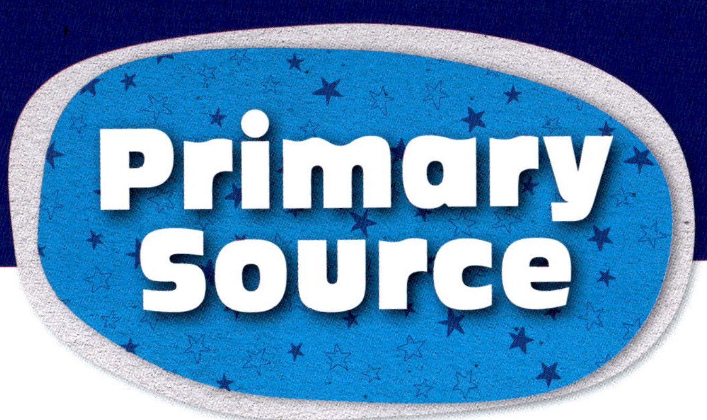

Grant Wood discussed how the Eldon house inspired his most famous painting:

> I saw a trim white cottage, with a trim white porch—a cottage built on severe Gothic lines. This gave me an idea . . . to find two people who, by their [stern and serious] characters, would fit into such a home.

Source: "*American Gothic*: Grant Wood's Midwestern Mystery." *Christie's*, 11 Dec. 2019, christies.com. Accessed 19 Sept. 2023.

Comparing Texts

Think about the quote. Does it support the information in this chapter? Or does it give a different perspective? Explain how in a few sentences.

Effigy Mounds National Monument protects mounds of earth made by people of the Woodland culture. These people lived in Iowa about 3,000 years ago.

CHAPTER 2

The People of Iowa

People have been living in Iowa for at least 11,000 years. By the 1600s, the Ioway (or Baxoje) and Dakota (or Sioux) were the two major American Indian peoples on this land. The Sauk (or Sac) and Meskwaki (or Fox) peoples came to Iowa in the 1700s.

European settlers also began to arrive in the 1700s. These settlers wanted land. By the 1850s, the US government had forced almost all American Indians out of Iowa. But the Sauk and Meskwaki peoples returned. They purchased land near Tama, Iowa. They had complete control over this land. The settlement grew over time. The Sac and Fox Tribe of the Mississippi in Iowa is now the state's only federally recognized tribe.

Today, less than 1 percent of Iowa's population is American Indian. About 84 percent is white. Black people make up 4.4 percent. Asian people are 2.8 percent. About 7 percent are Hispanic or Latino.

Meskwaki people often wear traditional clothing for celebrations today.

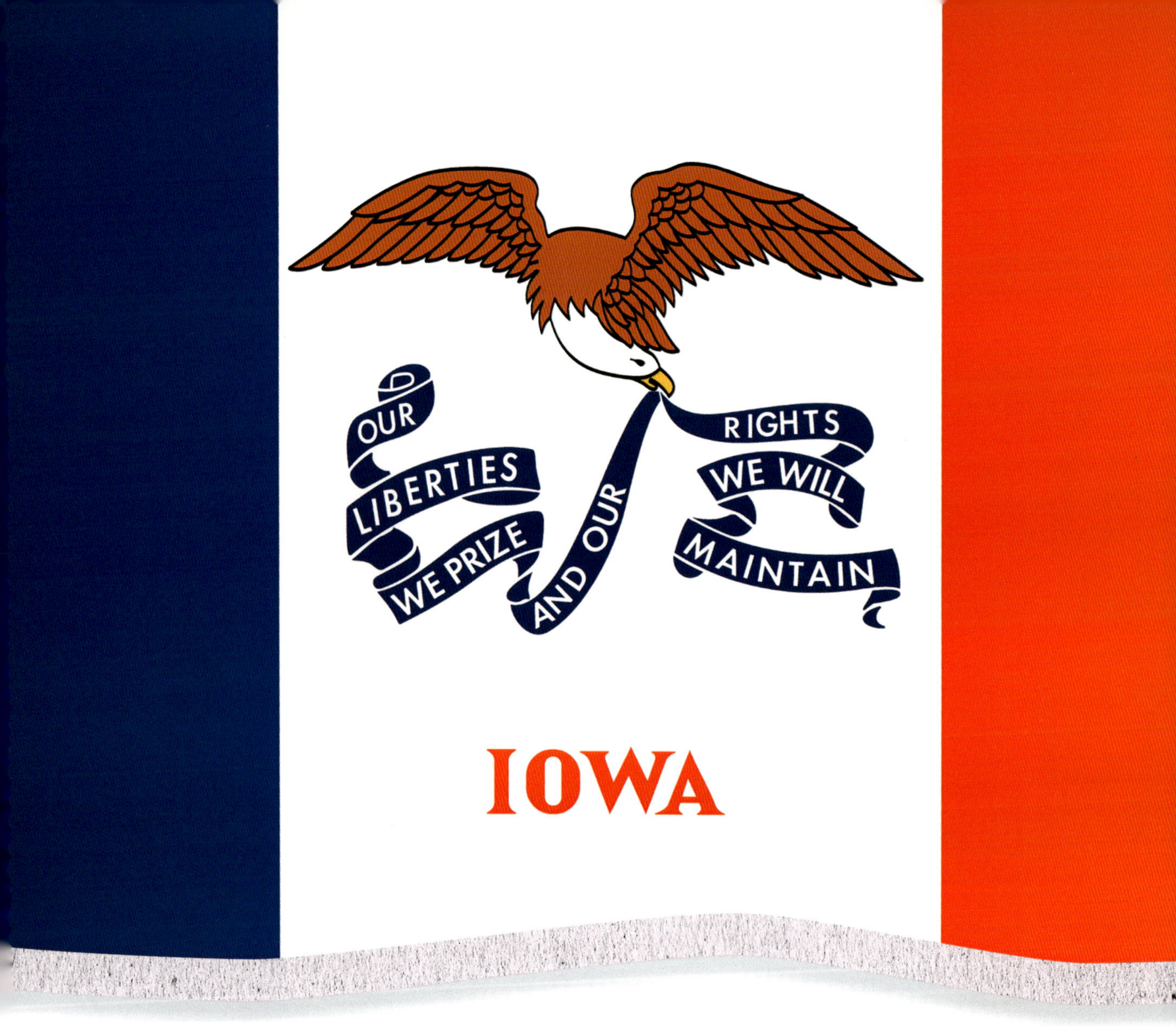

Iowa's state flag features a bald eagle and the state motto.

Life in Iowa

Iowa's **agriculture** is extremely important to the United States. Agricultural production in Iowa is second only to California. Iowa is the country's top producer of corn and hogs. Soybeans are another major crop.

More than 170 farmers markets are held throughout the state. At farmers markets, people can buy food directly from farmers. Sweet corn is an Iowa favorite.

Iowa State Fair

The Iowa State Fair is known for its delicious food. It is also known for butter. The Butter Cow sculpture is a major part of the fair. The sculpture is made from a metal frame and 600 pounds (270 kg) of butter. Since 1996, another sculpture has accompanied the cow every year. These have included pop culture icons and Iowan actors and athletes.

RAGBRAI riders spend eight days riding through many small towns in Iowa.

Manufacturing is another major Iowan industry. Iowan manufacturers make farm equipment, airplane parts, and much more. The state is also a leader in producing **ethanol** and wind energy. Other important industries in Iowa include health care and tourism.

Iowa has no major league sports teams. But college sports are a big deal in the state. Iowa has three public universities. Two of them have a strong rivalry. The Iowa Hawkeyes and Iowa

State Cyclones battle for the Cy-Hawk trophy every year.

Iowa is also home to a strong biking community. Every year, thousands of people join the Register's Annual Great Bicycle Ride Across Iowa (RAGBRAI). People from all over the world ride their bikes across the state. Every year is a new route. RAGBRAI showcases the food and hospitality of Iowa's towns.

Further Evidence

Look at the website below. Does it give any new evidence to support Chapter Two?

The Meskwaki Nation's History

abdocorelibrary.com/discovering-iowa

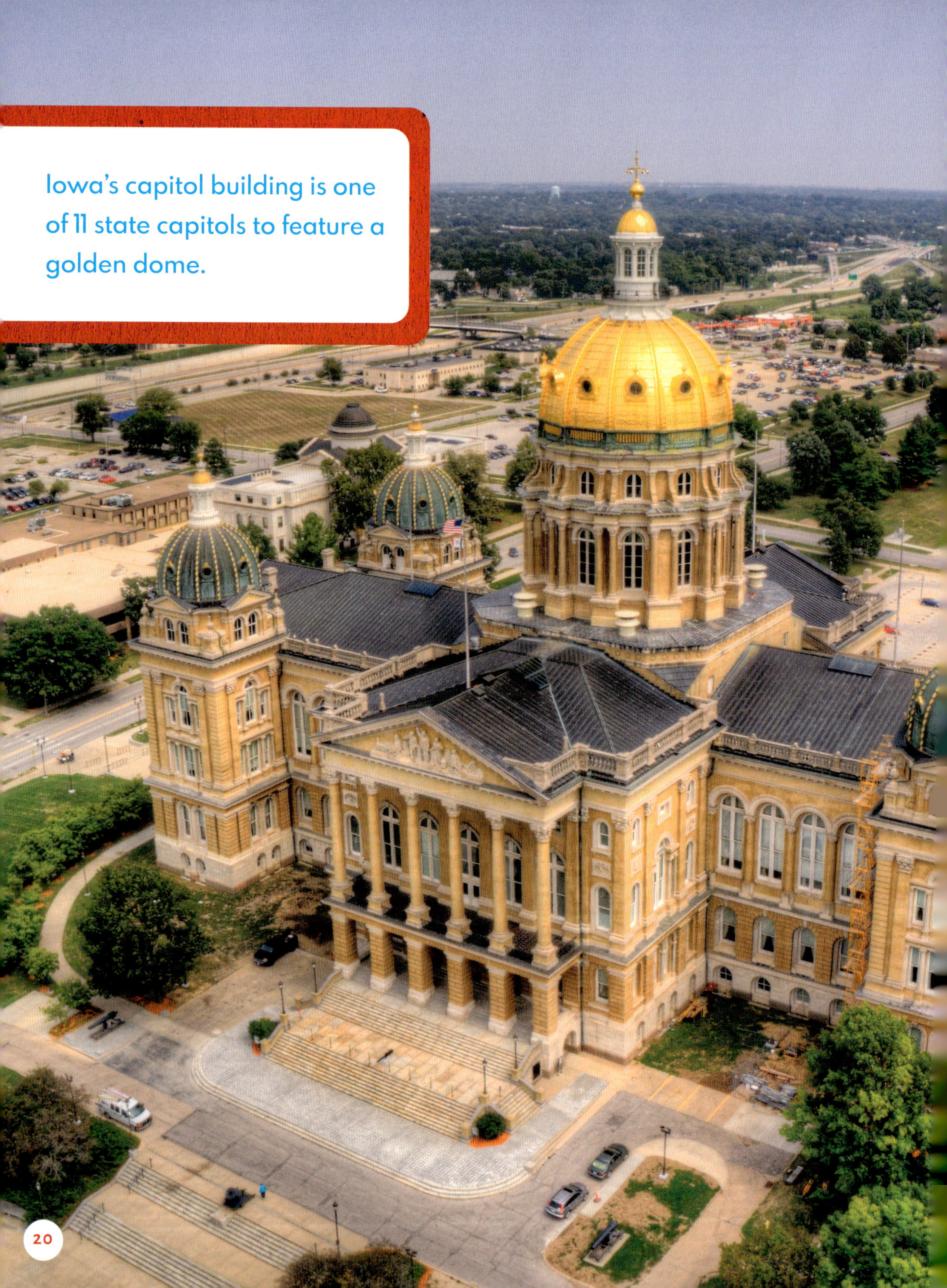

Iowa's capitol building is one of 11 state capitols to feature a golden dome.

CHAPTER 3

Places in Iowa

There are many places to explore in Iowa. Des Moines is Iowa's capital. It is also the largest city in Iowa. Visitors can tour the Iowa State Capitol building. Pappajohn Sculpture Park is in downtown Des Moines.

It is home to sculptures from more than two dozen artists.

Cedar Rapids is Iowa's second-largest city. People can visit Grant Wood's art studio. Many of Wood's paintings are displayed at the Cedar Rapids Museum of Art. Cedar Rapids is also home to the African American Museum of Iowa and the National Czech and Slovak Museum and Library.

In 2008, Iowa City became the world's third **UNESCO** City of Literature. The University of Iowa is in Iowa City. It is home to the first creative writing degree program in the United States. Many notable writers have graduated from the program. Iowa City has a strong literary culture.

Flannery O'Connor was a famous author. She graduated from the University of Iowa's creative writing program in 1947.

Natural Beauty

Western Iowa is home to the Loess (pronounced LUSS) Hills. Loess is a type of soil. Glaciers moved over this part of Iowa between 12,000 and 30,000 years ago. Then the glaciers melted. Wind blew the fine loess soil around. The soil formed bluffs and hills.

Effigy Mounds

Northeast Iowa is home to Effigy Mounds National Monument. The monument has more than 200 earthen mounds. People of the Woodland culture created the mounds. They lived in Iowa about 3,000 years ago. Some mounds are shaped like animals. Others are cone-shaped burial mounds. Effigy Mounds is considered a sacred space.

The Loess Hills have a shape similar to sand dunes.

Broken Kettle Grasslands Preserve is in the northern Loess Hills. This is Iowa's largest remaining native prairie. The rare prairie rattlesnake lives here. So does a herd of bison.

Iowa has something for all visitors to enjoy.

Twenty-eight bison were **reintroduced** to the prairie in 2008. By the 2020s, the herd had grown to more than 200.

The state that inspired Grant Wood's art remains a cherished home for many people. People enjoy Iowa's cities and its **rural** beauty. Its agriculture and manufacturing are important to the United States.

Explore Online

Visit the website below. Does it give any new information about prairies that wasn't in Chapter Three?

What Is a Prairie?

abdocorelibrary.com/discovering-iowa

American Gothic House

Loess Hills

Iowa: The Hawkeye State

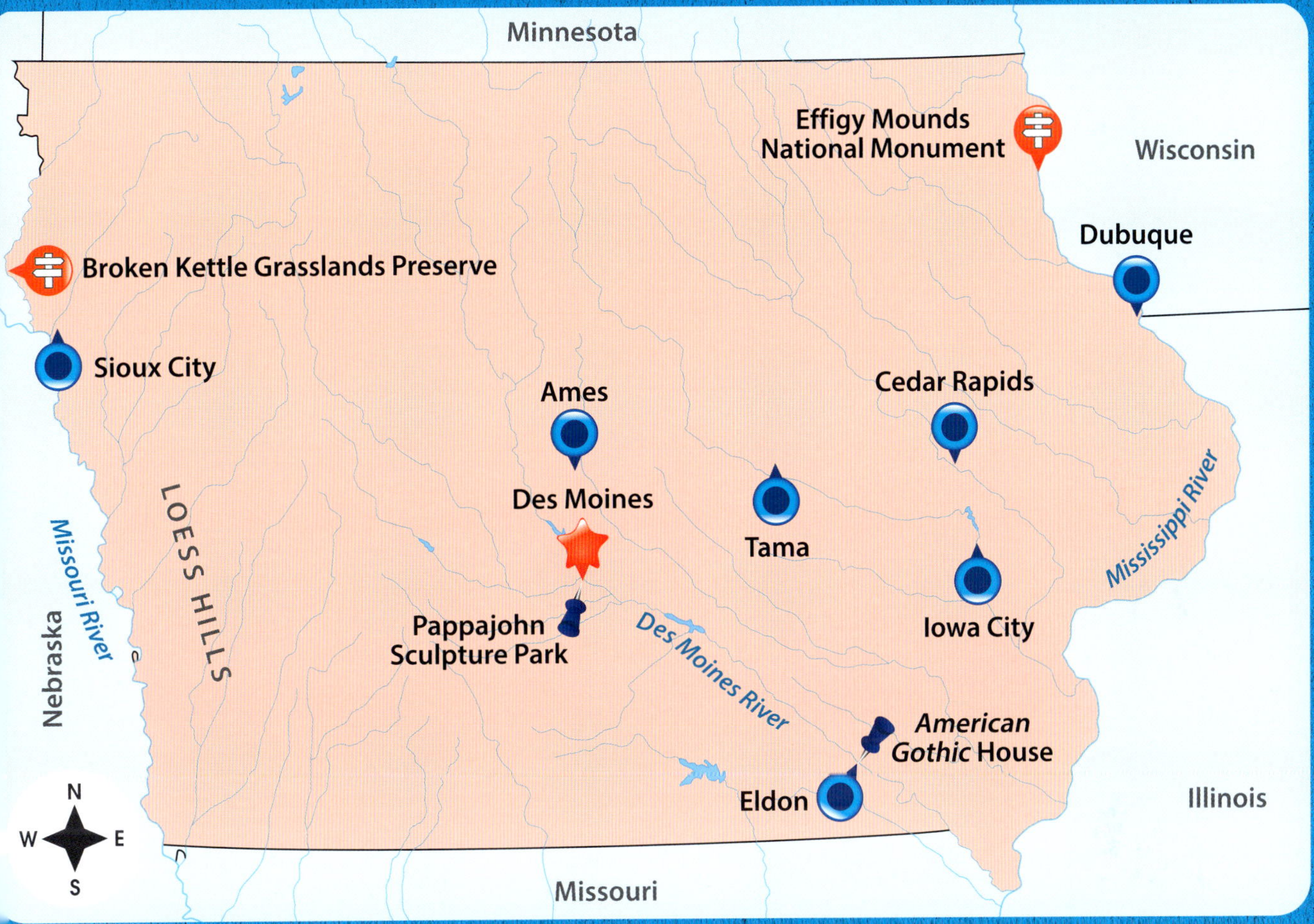

Minnesota
Effigy Mounds National Monument
Wisconsin
Dubuque
Broken Kettle Grasslands Preserve
Sioux City
Ames
Cedar Rapids
Des Moines
Tama
Mississippi River
Missouri River
LOESS HILLS
Nebraska
Pappajohn Sculpture Park
Des Moines River
Iowa City
American Gothic House
Eldon
Illinois
N
W
E
S
Missouri

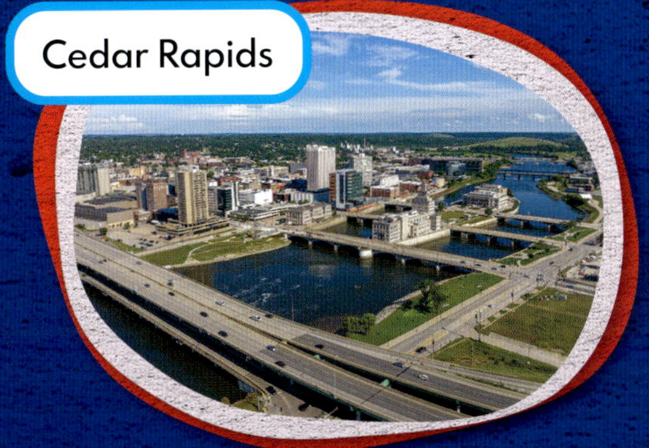

Cedar Rapids

Glossary

agriculture
farming

bluffs
steep hills, cliffs, or banks

ethanol
a type of fuel made from plants, including corn

humid
describing air that has a lot of moisture

manufacturing
the process of making goods to sell

reintroduced
brought back to an area

rural
relating to the countryside rather than the city

UNESCO
United Nations Educational, Scientific, and Cultural Organization, a group that identifies and protects natural and cultural heritage around the world

Online Resources

To learn more about Iowa, visit our free resource websites below.

Visit **abdocorelibrary.com** or scan this QR code for free Common Core resources for teachers and students, including vetted activities, multimedia, and booklinks, for deeper subject comprehension.

Visit **abdobooklinks.com** or scan this QR code for free additional online weblinks for further learning. These links are routinely monitored and updated to provide the most current information available.

Learn More

Hinman, Bonnie. *Farm Animals.* Abdo, 2023.

Murray, Julie. *Iowa.* Abdo, 2020.

National Geographic Kids United States Atlas. National Geographic, 2020.

Index

About the Author

K. A. Hale grew up in Cedar Rapids and graduated from Luther College in Decorah, Iowa. She now lives in Minnesota, where she writes, edits, and designs children's books. She visits her family in Iowa often, and she thinks nothing beats fresh Iowa sweet corn in the summer.